BLIMPS

A TRUE BOOK

by

Darlene Stille

Children's Press®
A Division of Grolier Publishing
New York London Hong Kong Sydney
Danbury, Connecticut

Reading Consultant
Linda Cornwell
Learning Resource Consultant
Indiana Department of
Education

**Blimps cause excitement
wherever they go.**

Library of Congress Cataloging-in-Publication Data

Stille, Darlene R.
  Blimps / by Darlene Stille
     p.   cm.
  Includes index.
  Summary: A simple explanation of blimps, airships that are lighter than
air, and how they have been used in both war and peace.
  ISBN 0-516-20327-4 (lib.bdg.) ISBN 0-516-26163-0 (pbk.)
  1. Airships—Juvenile literature. [1. Airships.] I. Title.
TL650.5.S75 1997
629.133'24—dc20
                                      96-28771
                                           CIP
                                          AC

Contents

Blimps are airships.

Lighter Than Air

A large round airship moves slowly across the sky. Everyone looks up at it. It can't be an airplane, because airplanes have wings and move fast. It can't be a helicopter, because helicopters have a large rotor. What is it?

It's a blimp! How can the blimp stay up in the sky? It is filled with a gas that is lighter than air.

A blimp is just like a birthday balloon that floats up—only bigger. Birthday balloons that float up must be held onto by a string. Let go of the string, and the balloon will float higher and higher until it disappears from view.

Balloons that float up are filled with a special gas called

These balloons are held up by helium gas.

helium. Helium is lighter than air. Balloons filled with air lie on the table or floor, because they weigh the same as the air around them. But balloons filled with helium will go up and up and up.

This truck carries helium tanks.

Blimps are also filled with helium. This makes blimps lighter than air and lets the blimps stay up in the sky.

Helium gas is pumped into the blimp (above). The helium gas gives the blimp shape and keeps it afloat (left).

The Parts of a Blimp

The blimp belongs to a group of vehicles called airships. All airships have big bags filled with gas that is lighter than air. The filled gas bags keep the airships afloat.

When a blimp is filled with gas, the gas makes the bag look firm and full. The gas

Drained of helium gas, a
blimp has no shape.

gives the blimp its shape.
When the gas is let out, it
becomes shapeless.

Long ago, airships had frames inside the gas bag. Frames were made of wood or metal. But blimps today do not have frames, because gas bags are made of sturdy fabric.

Under the gas bag is a place where the pilot sits. People who help the pilot also ride there. The pilot's helpers are called the crew. The place where the pilot and crew sit is called the gondola.

The blimp's crew sits in the gondola.

The pilot needs the fins to steer the blimp.

Engines for driving the blimp are attached to the gondola.

Fins stick out from the rear of the blimp. The fins have parts called elevators and rudders that help the pilot steer the blimp.

Steering a Blimp

It is time to take a ride on the blimp. The pilot and crew climb into the gondola. The pilot turns on the blimp's engines, which make the propellers turn. This moves the blimp through the air.

The pilot steers the blimp by using the elevators and

The pilot controls the blimp from inside the gondola.

the rudder on the fins. The elevators make the blimp's nose go up or down. The rudder makes the blimp turn right or left. These controls allow the pilot to move the blimp in any direction.

When the ride is over, it is time to take the blimp home. The blimp's home is a low tower called a mooring mast.

Workers on the ground catch hold of the blimp's ropes.

The pilot makes the blimp go down toward helpers on the ground near the mooring mast. There are ropes hanging from the blimp. The helpers grab the ropes and hold on tight so that the blimp cannot float away.

They tie the blimp to the mooring mast. With the blimp secured, the pilot and crew climb out of the gondola and down a ladder to the ground.

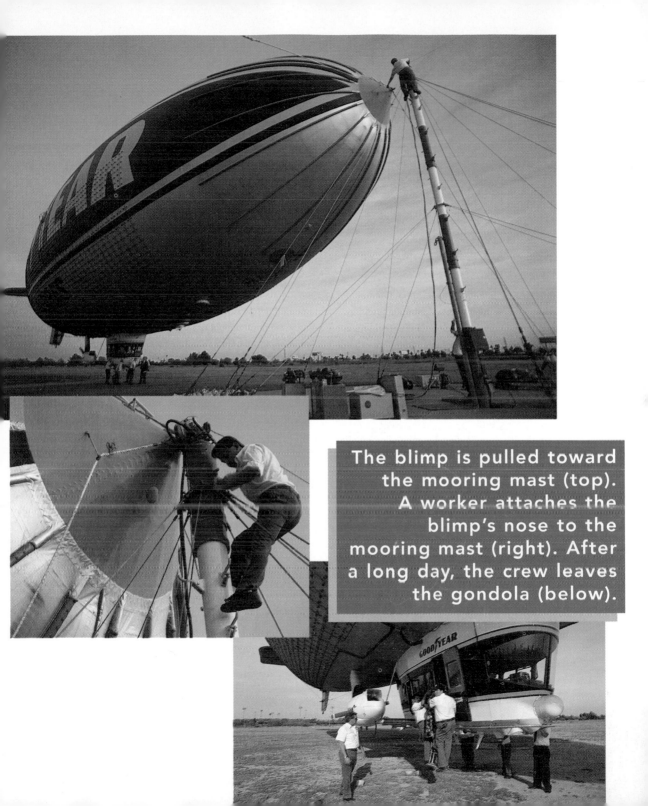

The blimp is pulled toward the mooring mast (top). A worker attaches the blimp's nose to the mooring mast (right). After a long day, the crew leaves the gondola (below).

The First Blimps

The idea of blimps came from balloons.

Balloons big enough to carry people were first made more than two hundred years ago. People rode in a basket that hung under the balloon.

The balloons were filled with hot air. Hot air is lighter

The first hot-air balloon flight was made in France on November 21, 1783.

than cold air, and this is what made the balloons go up. People still ride in hot-air balloons for fun.

Then inventors made gas balloons big enough to carry people. The gas they used was lighter than air. But they could not steer balloons. The balloons went wherever the wind took them.

The first true blimp was made in France. The gas bag was shaped like a football

and had an open basket hanging under it where people could ride. Attached to the basket was a steam engine to make the blimp move. The blimp also had a rudder. This blimp could be steered!

Blimp or Balloon?

What is the difference between a blimp and a balloon? Blimps are shaped long and narrow, like a football. Balloons are rounder, like a soccer ball. Balloons are also extremely difficult to steer. Blimps, however, have engines and fins that allow the pilot and crew to fly wherever they want.

Blimps are filled with helium, a gas that can keep it afloat for a long time. Balloons are filled with hot air. When the hot air inside the balloon cools, the balloon sinks to the ground.

People mostly fly balloons for fun. Blimps, however, are important for advertising and providing over-head shots at sports events.

With blimps, people could fly where they wanted to go.

Inventors then built bigger airships. They used frames of wood and metal for the big gas bags.

A German count named Ferdinand von Zeppelin built the biggest airships. They were longer than a football field. Count Zeppelin built the first passenger airship in 1909. This was before there were passenger airplanes. His

Count Zeppelin
built airships to
carry passengers.

airships were called zeppelins.
The zeppelins had cabins for
passengers under the gas bag.
People slept in the cabins
and ate in a dining room.

A zeppelin under construction (top).
Zeppelins were the largest airships ever built.

During the day, they looked at the scenery below and had a wonderful time. More than twenty thousand passengers flew in these airships.

Zeppelins used hydrogen gas to stay afloat. But hydrogen gas burned very easily. One small spark could cause the entire airship to explode. People thought airships were too dangerous. Soon more people flew in airplanes, and no more zeppelins were built.

The Hindenburg Disaster

The biggest zeppelin ever built was longer than two football fields. It was called the Hindenburg. The Hindenburg was filled

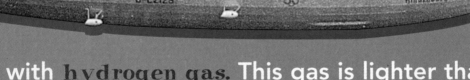

with hydrogen gas. This gas is lighter than air, but it can burn very easily. In 1937, the Hindenburg flew across the Atlantic Ocean and landed in New Jersey.

But just as it was coming to the mooring mast it **exploded and crashed,** killing many passengers and crew. The disaster convinced people that air travel in zeppelins was too dangerous.

The next day, burned and twisted metal was all that remained of the great airship.

Blimps in War

Before airplanes were invented, blimps were used in war. Generals wanted to see enemy soldiers. Was the enemy close? Would the soldiers attack?

The generals sent up blimps. Soldiers in blimps could see for miles. They could spot the enemy soldiers.

Blimps were a common sight during World War I.

This Navy blimp searches for submarines.

Sailors in blimps looked for enemy ships. Blimps over the ocean looked for submarines.

Soldiers and sailors used blimps in World War I (1914–1918). German zeppelins flew over England during World War I and dropped bombs. But the bombs were very small, and they did little damage.

After World War I, airplanes replaced blimps in war.

Blimps Today

Blimps today are safe. They are filled with helium, which is safer than hydrogen. Helium cannot burn or explode.

Most blimps today are used for advertising. Football fans can look up and see a blimp above the stadium. Baseball fans can look up and see a blimp above the ballpark.

Today, blimps are a common sight at sports events.

These two blimps advertise tires.

Many blimps are decorated with pictures and words. Blimps carry advertisements on their gas bag for products such as tires or film. Ads written on blimps can be seen by millions of people.

Blimps also provide special camera shots. People watching a game on television can see a picture of the action far below. The picture comes from television cameras on the blimp.

This photograph of the Indianapolis 500 driving race was taken from a blimp.

Blimps Tomorrow

Will there be new jobs for blimps? Some people think so.

Huge blimps can carry heavy loads. They could also be used to lift cars and trucks and even big machines.

Big blimps could carry passengers to places that are difficult—or impossible—to

Blimps can travel over difficult terrain, such as a rain forest.

reach by airplane, boat, train, or motor vehicle. Blimps might carry tourists on sight-seeing trips to tropical rain forests or to tall mountains. They might take visitors or equipment to the North or South Pole.

Scientists could use blimps for research. They could look for animals from a blimp or check for air pollution up high. They could look for signs of pollution in lakes and rivers.

The future may hold many new jobs for blimps.

In the future, there might be many jobs for big blimps.

To Find Out More

Here are some additional sources to help you learn more about blimps.

 **Books**

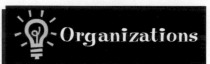 **Organizations**

Berliner, Don. **Before the Wright Brothers.** Lerner, 1990.

Gibbons, Gail. **Flying.** Holiday, 1986.

Johnson, Niel. **Fire and Silk: Flying in a Hot Air Balloon.** Little, 1990.

Munro, Roxie. **Blimps.** Dutton, 1988.

Stein, R. Conrad. **The Hindenburg Disaster.** Children's Press, 1993.

Airship Association - U.S.
8512 Cedar Street
Silver Springs, Maryland 20910

Balloon Federation of America
P.O. Box 400
Indianola, Iowa 50125

Online Sites

Airship and Blimp Resources

http://www.amherst.edu/ ~rkescher/airship.html

Lists organizations and other websites concerned with airships.

Airship

http://spot.colorado.edu/ ~dziadeck/airship.html

Provides information and a discussion page on Zeppelins and other airships.

Balloon Life's World Wide Web Page

http:www.aero.com/ publications/balloon_life/ bl.htm

Gives information about recreational ballooning.

World Wide Blimp Page

http://alf.zfn.uni-bremen.de/ ~ronald/blimp/wwblimp .html

Important Words

airship aircraft that uses lighter-than-air gas to fly

elevator movable part on a blimp's fins that help the pilot steer up or down

gondola cabin attached to the underside of a blimp

helium gas that is lighter than air

hydrogen gas that is lighter than air but can explode easily

mooring mast small tower where blimps land

rudder movable part on a blimp's fins that steer right or left

zeppelins gigantic airships built from 1909 to 1937

Index

Meet the Author

Darlene Stille resides in Chicago and is executive editor of the *World Book Annuals.* She has written several Children's Press books, including *Extraordinary Women Scientists,* *Extraordinary Women of Medicine,* and four other True Books on transportation.